Rumor of Cortez

Rumor of Cortez

poetry by

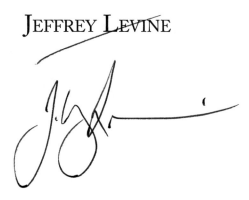

JEFFREY LEVINE

Red Hen Press ❧ Los Angeles

Rumor of Cortez

Book design by Michael Vukadinovich
Cover art by William Kuch, WK Graphic Design

ISBN: 1-59709-004-2

Library of Congress Catalog Card Number: 2004118152

Published by Red Hen Press

The City of Los Angeles Cultural Affairs Department, California Arts
Council, Los Angeles County Arts Commission and National Endow-
ment for the Arts partially support Red Hen Press.

First Edition

Acknowledgments

Grateful acknowledgment is made to the publications in which most of these poems first appeared, sometimes in different form:

American Letters & Commentary, *Ascent*, *Barrow Street*, *Blaze* (online), *GSU Review*, *In Posse*, *The Journal*, *Melange*, *Mississippi Review*, *New Orleans Review*, *North American Review*, *Notre Dame Review*, *Now Culture*, *Pleiades*, *Rattapallax*, *Slope*, *The Drunken Boat*, *3ʳᵈ Bed*, *Three Candles*, and *The Virginia Quarterly Review*.

Abounding thanks to:
the *Mississippi Review* and Angela Ball for awarding "Orpheus Ascending" first prize in the 2001 Mississippi Review Poetry Competition, and *North American Review* and Yusef Komunyakaa for awarding "Mazurka" the James Hearst Poetry Prize.

With special gratitude to those who have so well sustained, closely read, thoughtfully mulled, and brilliantly availed with loving kindness: Susan Dineen, Laurie Stoll Grimshaw, Roy Jacobstein, Ronni Leopold, Grace Dane Mazur, Susan R. Williamson, and that visionary, apostle of opacity, Prince of Hearts, Ilya Kaminsky. Wildflowers, especially, to Kate Gale, Mark Cull, and Red Hen Press.

To Nena, Alexander, and the outermost reaches of my family

♓

Contents

César could shave the rind from any assertion to expose its pulp and jelly. But César was otherwise ruled by pulp. César loved everything that ripened in time.

—Richard Rodriguez, *Days of Obligation*

And I admit that reason stands confounded in presence of the veritable prodigy that love is . . .

—Marguerite Yourcenar, *Memoirs of Hadrian*

I

♓

Rumor of Cortez

Hardly a clever soigné beauty like what's her name,
the ideal choice for a man of my constrained austerity.
What colossal tortures we will not endure!

Maybe take a few days to think this over.
I have a theory. It's only a theory, but I'd bet on it.
Each of us does nothing to lighten the journey.

There's, for example, the dog. Deadbeat
expatriate, aimless loser. Sure. But there was a time
I had an assignment. A man, a woman, a dog, a young boy.

The woman, ankle-length taffeta dress, sea breezes teased
the skirt. The man, the boy, the skirt, the dog. The dog
shimmering with liquid crystals of ocean and the stick

he has retrieved, good boy!, the boy's throw, or the man's.
Who can tell from here? *Carissimo!* she calls,
her voice like wind chimes. That's how we met.

There on the sidewalk. Downtown. I thought she meant the Brit
married to the Swedish chemicals tycoon. *Darling! Pumpkin!*
Quickly, I ordered toast with orange marmalade—

champagne in a black bottle. But enough about my morals.
"Lend me some cuttings; I have barren land."
She spoke in semicolons, quickly she accused me.

So I said, little pink and turquoise pills are the impossible details
of my life. And for some reason, I don't float. We tackled
the problem of recollection. Decided to import tables,

tiger maple armoires, little ceramic pieces from Manzanillo.
How about an ancient jeep from the valet at the Four Seasons,
the guy with the spider tattoo. Take a little tent. Ignore

the rumors of Cortez. Pop the turquoise pills with white rum.
Turquoise shells and silver water. We could look to the dog
for motivation. Reconfigure the driftwood. Roll our own

tortillas of amaranth dough over the skulls of our enemies,
like the Aztecs: She of the Jade Skirt: Goddess of the Waters.
Huixtotin Lady: Goddess of Salt. Let's run the lines again.

I forget now whose idea it was. And the little boy
in the sailor suit, chucking driftwood, lathing
into hunter, feather worker, goldsmith, potter, scribe.

Mazurka

I was selling tulip bulbs smuggled in from Holland.
A kind of circus in the back alleys, past
lime-white cottages with thatched roofs below Bratislava,
mellow peaches on the trees in the reddish-yellow approach
of summer evening. Peony Tulip Angelique, Marvel and Obdam
Narcissus, the rare Praestans Fusilier, Darwin Snow Peaks.

Of these tulips—so profound, serenity
I've learned to say in five languages, seven dialects.
I could say other things by memory:
Perhaps the electron is neither particle nor wave,
but grief instead, a dissonance, less simple.

This I say in English, the tulips go even faster.
Next to me a peasant hawked his oblong, blue-black eggs.
Music frightens the oxen, he said, in Czech.
And then in English, the single word, "pathetic,"
his accent in all three syllables like a relief map
of pressure zones and granite.

He hummed an old mazurka to his even older horse,
damp nostrils trembling, flanks sweating
manganese and iron oxide, odor of subterranean stone,
while I fed the roan bulb after bulb from my open palm.

Henri of Hoboken, an Epic

Following his much-celebrated debut, *Dante at Large*, the Poet returns with another enduring hero. This time it's a fifty-year-old Gnostic with a photographic memory. Henri's intermittently reared by gamblers, thieves, whores and priests in one of America's most notorious sin cities. But, he's living as a saint in fifth century Byzantium.

As in *Dante at Large*, the Poet's new epic describes the labyrinthine terrain in which we shape our identities and search for meaning. And like Dante, mid-life Henri places his questions into a distant and possibly wiser world. For some reason, the stories of ancient Byzantium help Henri make sense of his absurd—and often dangerous—existence. *Henri of Hoboken* is an ironic, funny, and heart-rending account of the ways we become our own saviors by choosing what to believe.

Praise for *Dante at Large*

". . . a charming, unexpectedly poignant first epic."
                    —*The Willamette Picayune*

"*Dante at Large* is a work of art that struts its way on to the bookshelf . . ."
                    —*Clearwater Beacon*

". . . a modestly entertaining poem."
                    —*The New Jersey Post Book World*

Excerpts from *Henri*—

Henri went to bed and lay down. He tried to forget himself and Byzantium and Hoboken. To forget everything, but he couldn't. He went to the window and challenged the darkness. He knew this was a cliché. He didn't care anymore.

His angel said, those who come to know themselves enjoy their possessions. Henri asked the angel what happened if you had nothing to possess, his face pressed to the glass, trying to see the empty fields below.

The angel said, then the light will descend upon you and you will be clothed in it. The angel spoke like this.

Henri tried to imagine being clothed in light, but he couldn't. He was disappointed. It was like that sometimes. He would go instead to the mountains of New Hampshire, start there. He would take a new lover. They'd walk. It would be many days. They'd hold each other's faces with both hands. They'd throw away their clothes, see what happened in the light. Or swim to Byzantium. Lay off the angel. Lay down in the ivory sand.

Prophet Plant

That's how you know she's in the kitchen
baking honey cake, pouring in another
cup of bees, my Nana, Anna, her summer, house
on the edge of everywhere, on the bluegrass, world's roof,
campion bladder moss. Her cinquefoil and sweet coltsfoot binding
winter. Her blessings: cowberry, mountain
cranberry, cottongrass, see—

dwarf birch in flower, *Betula nana*, prophet plant,
so that is how you know
she's in the kitchen, my braveheart,
but wary of lupine, and why not? bastard
plant, choking out the oxytrope,
the saxifrage or bullying up the baby
mountain sorrel. So, Anna, my Nana,
just now brewed a cup of Labrador tea
for my Poppy the pattern cutter, here, have
some, even if they'd not meet before the boat,
before the bow, she'd be ready with her stories, the arctic
willow white between her breasts, making him say it:
Cassiope tetragona,
making him say it again.

According to the polar reports,

there is no grief. Too cold for that. Still, age after age,
the high-flying prow nears Polaris. It is enough to steer
by the twilight reds of achiote and carmine.

Nothing lasts a hundred years, not even paradise.
I give up mine. Flood the dining room with sunlight.

In the mountains as I passed a flock of sheep
in the midday heat, it was possible to know with certainty,
this was not the first time I have lived. But I was wrong.
Our swimming on moonlit nights is all the counterproof I need.
(The dining room was witchcraft, or a dream.)

Let's gather the equipment, see the landscape.
We'll pack one tent for our love, another for our sins, walk south
until we can hold each other steady—until we find courtyards
trimmed with lemon trees.

Here's an Audubon of birdcalls, bells, all bells.
It grows cold—molted duck feathers wash up
in great heaps, on the beach.

A flock of snow geese rises, a snowstorm.
(Everybody catches something that disappears.)

To make this for you, sweet seer,

I say cold are the great cold walls of your temples
and your cold cities, and they burst out laughing.

I say mornings fill with migrant birds flowing
just above the waves, the tropics in their feathers,

the heron wheels and shrieks, circles the pond—
such is the heart—one forgets the blinds of midnight.

This is the body saved from the sea. Think instead
of Paris in winter, a baker slips the first tray of croissants

from the oven as street lamps flicker out along the Seine,
and no one yet on the Boulevard des Capuccines.

Lovers pull up heavy blankets, sleep—while in the village,
a lone farmer brings in the hay, his chickens dusted with snow.

Winter sky, roofs and shutters, shrubs and picket fences
flocked winter white. Winter. And something about madness.

As for the sea, each shell is a leftover soul, frozen, hard
as amber, opaque as amber. That is what you hear—

the sea lends a frieze, the waves a body—
a sea bird, a sea woman, night, a piece of quartz.

The beach buries itself under a foot of questions,
the water tastes them inch by inch.

There's so much it is better not to know.
If only sunflowers would grow inside my bedroom.

Here's another place I do not belong,
much as I love your red dress, a good cry.

My Antonia

At heart, we're all pets, every one of us the soft fossil print
of utter devotion, a dog, say, or the dog in a story about a dog,
or the story of a dog locked in inside a memory of a dog—

paws pressed to the chest—first there's the trick of unconditional
love, and then the ink of things spills over the white of things.
We tease ourselves with possibility because we can't help

counting the stones and counting the days and counting
the heartbeats and the widening spaces between. It's okay.
Some days you can count on the counting.

Doesn't matter how many times you climb,
you never trust the rungs, not once, not ever, how could you?
And still you climb and fall, climb and fall—

dumbstruck—goofy smile, sad eyes, addled
heart and a pocket full of ripe blackberries
that someone handed you or you pilfered

from the street market, those tiny, plump-faced gods
dyeing your tongue blue and sweet. It's all praise of a kind—
belief, disbelief, sobbing, loving, the small clear charities.

One day you hear music, your leg starts thumping
and you let go of the universe, it spins off into wherever
the universe goes when you stop thinking about it,

stop fixing it to your thoughts—and the sun is so bright
and the air so clear you dive down into it while holding
someone's hand in your mouth, my hand, mortise and tenon,

tongue and groove. Here, let me stroke those ears again.
Let me smooth your flanks, that silk, with my clumsy fingers.
In our country the only currency, my best girl, is longing.

Antonia, Pearl Fisher

Antonia, my sweet golden, is a great pearl fisher.
You should see her dive, muzzle oddments from the ocean floor,
send them free floating up to me like untroubled fates.

First we build ourselves a shrine to the goddess
of oysters, like a little diorama-box whittled
from an old oar handle. We offer sacrificial gifts

of crabs and eels, kelp drawings on the rocks,
grab bags of celestial music. How well
this celestial music travels under water!

Submerged, in canine ecstasy, Antonia outthinks Descartes.
Je suis, ergo je swim. Occasionally, just to be politic,
he does a little dance for the smaller gods

who miss the markets, who know one's home fills
with true hard things and has shape, gold chalices,
the helmets, the crowns, the pikes and halberds,

his swashbuckled armor, glittering like sunfish.
We have our ceremonies—Antonia insists on ritual—
first deep thinking, then dancing, then the pearls.

There's a Hole in the Screen

The night has disappeared into my cat.

She carries the message in her teeth.
In the dark, few are in love, many breathe.

Bach was right. Joy is all in the desiring. Oh Eve! There was blood on my hands, a broken glass, a million shards, a dozen wounds. There, a quill, an inkwell filled with spores from which grow fugues. They lie in state. One touches them, that's all.

Make a note. Plant next time no annuals. How they suffer up your *freude!* Basso. Contralto. Duo. What's present are many of the insteads. It is not too late to wonder about them. There is one now, suspended in the bilious wind. Bilious. Take a reef. Hard alee.

Okay. Inclusion is profligate. Omission offers up its own rewards. Take another reef. Reach.

Well, enough of figurative passions. I have never been defeated so completely. If a fog can be light, then I am ready to return to my kabbalist. He who sanctifies the exalted, and so on. Lest your attention go grievous, I have bandaged up my hand. You there. Above.

The fog burns off, I am told, each morning. Here is a morning, fog facing east. Your face in it. Desire, I say. Justification, I say, and mean of course in canticles, I love, you love, they love.

Dove?

Word.

Unword.

Punkawallahs

What a surly coddled clot of insolent self-aggrandizers. And madmen.
That too.

Isaiah, Jeremiah, Ezekiel especially, that apocalyptic whiz kid brigand.
Hawkers, rickshaw pullers, punkawallahs, boat-builders all.

Do you think I watch you only when you pray, turn away when you toss
your worthless coins in your pagan fountains? Maybe I'm up there
sunning myself on the moons of Uranus, equatorial Oberon, the southern
coast of Umbriel.

So, my prophets, my loves, you must never say the world bears my
sacrifice, nor tell a soul the Earth's eye's gone indiscreet, knees more
quaked.

Say instead, the edges of the world blur to silhouette, even as you wait
beside the window, having finished with your garden, each globe of fruit
on its slender stalk. You cannot move even as the city lightens, the sky
clear as nitrogen, brittle as toast.

II

♓

The World Dissolves

We fail every time at surprise.
When you lose yourself, you face south-southwest
like the caged bird. It can't be helped.
In the field, something licks dew from the autumn grass
before the shoots return to frost. Somewhere the sun
spends its flame, the sky shatters through its glass.
At certain hours of the day, your body floods
with instinct, so much of you having been entered.

Limbs follow when you lie down,
a shadow of your own, curving to every curve
like the Hebrew alphabet into Greek, letters cross
the page, greet each other mid-history, bent
under the heft of familiar cargoes, the sorrows,
the collective hope of cells, call it, or bare faith of the body.

Continental Breakfast for Two

I've set the morning table for you. Linen,
the good silver, silver coffee urn, coffee in the urn,
the cornflowers straight up like wings or drooped
like wings, and some favorite napkin rings, the ones
from Bali made of light, lighter, lightest
wood and painted bright
in the Balinese style by eight child
painters who do not live at home.

My voice is lower in the morning.
You should know this so it doesn't frighten off
the angels, and I speak in breathy phrases—
but this is all ritual, I swear, not for hurt.
First thing, I check the radio for life.
If it's news—it's always news—I turn it off again
because the story is about tunnels,
the coming ice age or algae bloom,
and with it, that new problem without a cure—
not even a single name or even a good photo.

Oh mysterious pulse.
You will have had your nightmares
and your flannel gowns to warm them—
go ahead, you won't be sorry. Take
the lemon marmalade, spread some murmur
about courage under it, and count
in pairs the ribs missing on both sides,
so it's not a creation thing, you understand.

Fold back the paper as if
it were printed in Chinese ink,
as if it were all about Sundays or quills
or new passages from the orient, or
how the story continues on a page
someone didn't think to keep.

As the waiter refills the catsup,

we want to know more about, of all things, all things. Well, hell.
Forgive us, for we know not what we ask.

Look, I'm still holding on to my spoon, and on to hunger, you say,
consoling, I say, I'd turn on myself if a story could explain
the heart's version of the facts, and face it, love is almost love enough—

that's how it is and damn the sky, all of it, damn the half-bitten moon
and damn its dim-witted light, damn the promises and the incompetence
of stars and damn that riders snap to attention where the bay curves
against its will and the lights with it—

                    But love is not the point. In particular,
that thing happened again in your eyes, though you said no, then yes.

How often have we seen this? as the waiter sizes up the condiments,
sweeps to the floor our shared crumbs and sets down those heavy white cups,
each one with a telling thwunk—half-and-half?

I do not mean to say that everything is lost—far from it—and anyway,
we can dance, and should, and do, right there in the diner, past the bus stand
and the tired cook and the traveler who cannot read his map.

Sea Light

Now this world resembles every other,
we notice this each day in our bright
questions without waiting for an answer.
What more does anybody need to know?
asks my neighbor, come home to find, mid-summer,
his young wife burning someone's letters on the grill.

Well, I could just as easily be wrong. Swears
he's seen the same twilight at the movies,
and I don't know whether he means sea light—
he is not the sort of man to notice
sea light in the suburbs (else it could have been
one of those heat mirages). No ocean for at least
a hundred miles—it is only reflection, one more stab
at the heart's hat-full of tricks—if it seems that sea light fills
the western line of houses out beyond his lawn.

Even the Smallest Hesitation

Everything, once, was worthy of belief.
Your hands fell inarticulate with joy, remember?

If it snowed, it must have been cold.
If the snow melted, the day must have warmed
in the afternoon sun,
maybe spring had come, who knows?

Even now, one blows kisses at the heavens
as the clouds part. Obedient clouds.

So, when at night lying on your back
with your eyes wide open and the moonlight
in them, trying to remember the coincidence
of telling her yes, you loved her,
and at the same moment meaning it,
it may have sounded, you'll admit,
peremptory, your hands (remember) inarticulate with joy.

To Sleep

"I've given it up," my lover writes
as resignation is her job and therefore mine,
she's seen me here, eyewitness, swears
she's watched one night's sky, a constellation of minarets,
owing its incompletion to the short memory of saints—
because saints must be so possessed, she knows
their names and lineage, their coats of arms—
What saints are these? open, cloaks fluttering
so to trick the night—that she hears the holy,
dreamless, their blessings rise unfeathered
as my own sleep (and therefore hers) seeps past the door.
Give us a drama, a scattering of birds
loosed from the aviary—motiveless, instinctual,
a flight unmarred by clues, bell through cloud.
Even the privileged do not live as we have done.
Sweet angel of a thousand sleepless turns,
stay awhile, I beg her, (*quickly now—*
we're running out of servants, out of port)
stay this frayed, moth-eaten night.

The Color of Cardinals

As allowing for passage through a certain kind of incandescence—
things disappear—they disappear and with them, conventional
itineraries, subterranean walls, passion-fruit or the unwound string,
and better, the last half note of your favorite Brandenburg, or best,
the weathered skin of the old men up in the hills,
what they drink, what they wear around their necks,
(the color of your lips) (the color of theirs) what they think or anyway,
that pigment in the desert cliffs, up there toward the top and in them,
nearly visible in the first blush of morning, the stunned red birds.

Morning, Orient Point

Clear as late October rose, scent of pumpkins from forgotten fields,
ones the pickers left behind for luck as they moved through the furrows,

or left because their shapes suggest what field hands wanted to forget—

the farms you pass mid-winter, seized with rime and solid earth, plow
blade at ease on the drive, the old tractor chained to a post like a workhorse,
patient and alone, while passing headlights carve out country scenes—
dreams of spring—drooping boughs, dripping leaves. Stone church, rail
fence, fireplug.

By the river three rusted-out and battered barges lie cabled to the pier.
Past the planking, a staircase rises to the upper deck where I'll take my
place beside the rail. One orange, one loaf of day-old peasant bread, and
high tide dazes even the largest stones.

Each year something drops from the sky, spreads its wings, enormous on
the field, while farm dogs whine and sniff the air.

Testament

In this hemisphere the choices are all bright silver
and submerged, or pale blue with cherry-colored fins
on Limoges, a platter of saffron breads and scarlet snouts.

To illustrate: somewhere deep in the interior,
there was a waterfall and ripe vegetation—coconuts
and banana trees, nameless plants with star-shaped trunks,

tips sharp as blades—and don't forget the flying foxes, the wild pigs.
Back by the water's edge, all manner of delicacies: white flesh, soft and flat,
spoiled in the sun's heat and unspoiled in the cool of night.

One employs false methods, takes liberties, smashes
into everything, the eager heart goes blind. You leave the world
to its broad daylight.

You're cheating. It's a crime, but isn't it a kind of glory?
You do it because love adores, it burns inside you,
and with it, the water burns like a sulfur torch.

III

Comprimario

Chopin decided to travel blind.
What use are maps to someone who knows
his place does not know him? Let me explain.
The words "his place does not know him"
so beguiled Chopin that he whispered them
again and again, his right hand resting
on the keyboard. Suddenly illuminated,
he saw phrases enfold around the broken
edges of arpeggios, around scales scattered
like dried sea grass in the tidal pools—
away from the guesthouse with its strings
and hammers, far from his bedroom
with its southern light.

From his villa in Mallorca Chopin wrote,
"I caught cold in spite of the heat, palms, figs,
and the three most famous doctors on the island.
One said I had died, the second, that I am dying,
the third that I shall die."

When one is ready to leave, even a single
wooden spoon is enough to stir the world.
Add a colander, a perfect paring knife,
or row upon row of ivory keys, tempered
and sweet, the heart wills itself to break.

Expulsion

Fact is, she was mad with boredom.
Adam, too, though less so. You know how it is with men.
He could have stayed longer, a few years anyway, but still,
he found himself imagining Eve *with* clothes,
maybe some lingerie or a black dress, and too,
he wondered how the lamb might taste slow roasted on a spit
over a rhododendron fire, basted with red wine,
and he had no red wine. None. And Eve.

Well. There was the brook just beyond the Garden.
She could hear it. It sang to her close up like the willow ptarmigan,
it lowed from far away like the caribou.
She wanted to bathe in it, had to, though in truth,
water enough flowed through the Garden, some below ground,
like the caves of the Baja, and some above,
catching in deep pools where it teased Eve with her reflection
and the reflection of distant clouds.

It was there she named so much she was denied,
though she knew denial to be a cavil.
Who would not want to see loons and Greenland parrots,
puffins and Mother Carey's chickens, Leach's storm-petrels,
black guillemots, an Arctic sky suffused with swallows?
And what about the bottomless Norwegian sun,
the northern people: Yup'ik and Inupiat?

What of them? Given time, even something vast appeals,
even something barren.

Dreaming in Hobson-Jobson

If I bring you bags of salt like the Danaquils to Ahmed
the Left-Handed, it is so I can settle peacefully in ancient Harar,
not as writer but farmer. Why? Because I've not yet dreamed
a single line. Not one, but will. Nor seen men feeding

the hyenas each evening in the old khasba. Men who know nothing
of danger proper, though some are missing fingers, and others, hands.
If, dear one, I confuse my powers with my dreams, know also
that you, too, compose the best part of my dreamlife, are so composed.

Like the Pin-tailed Whydah, the Shropshire Terrier, the thick bolt
of Dacron—mine or not—they're mine to dream, and, woman,
you'd best pray I don't wake up! Still, my love, you are as lovely
east of Eden as ever you were west. Taking our sons

to a double feature now: they're already talking about Milk Duds,
the taste of Harar's salt on their popcorn. And that Cain—
this morning griping to know why I take little Abel in my arms
when we cross the highway. Maybe this will mollify

though, I confess, I want to muss his hair less and less.
After, maybe you could take them swimming for a while.
I'll make you a quick river. I've gardening to do,
hoes to sharpen, ground to break.

Sweet Cheat

Eve sleeps with arms behind her head, movie star,
posed for the camera, and her mouth moves

with slow words and unknown murmurs
in a low register—sounds like a cello or the night-purring

of the lioness. Her muffled snoring comforts him.
She in the red silk nightie he gave her following the expulsion,

which she wears to remind herself that even the snake wanted her.
Even the heron. Her dark hair covers one eye, and drapes

in folds across her collarbone, her breastbone, her ribs.
He has so often confused waking and dreaming that this,

he knows, is not his, not even hers, and besides, see the twin
patches of tender skin beneath both eyes, bruised plums.

Looking at Eve, he does not ask himself what art is.
Thinks of the way Swann holds off before kissing

Odette, and still has no notion of art, nor of sacrifice,
only the background pulse of the momentous.

Thinks, there is nothing careful here—we've been greedy,
we've been tithed. Gets up. The kitchen bulb flickers—

long broken. Adam grumbles at the toaster, the sink,
coffee on the cups stacked in the sink, three-days'-worth.

The lipstick on her cup, which he lifts, carmine stain
to his closed eye, the one he cannot open, has not since

he first heard about the boy. He pours himself a glass of juice.
No pulp. The kind the boy liked. There are no madeleines

in the pantry. Not even sure what a madeleine is,
has no nuance to hold this detail in perspective.

In the boy's room, the closet door open, robes hang down,
and a book with a brilliant-colored cover lies face-up upon the bed.

The boy's book, Adam switches on the bed lamp, the mattress exhales
as he sits. He has forgotten to drink his orange juice.

The glass is in his hand, or he has left it somewhere,
or he has left it nowhere. The boy's book is a fantasy,

he remembers: witty, he remembers, made his boy laugh,
he remembers, there's a bookmark where they left off.

Adam starts to read. The book is full of sly jokes,
each one another runty piss-ant little pistol,

each nothing-caliber bullet, each one
another sweet cheat gone.

Orange Birds at Tulum

And what's more, I went on, ready to commit any number
of improprieties to shake that awkward silence,
you're left-handed, aren't you? I asked my Eve, filling
page after page with Palmer Method script.

Her lips curled at the corners, but her gaze remained
distant, remote, circumspect, filled with irreducible resolve.
I offered her a glossary of new poses: a drop-dead glance,
arms wrapped snugly about her knees. Or a trial phrase.

There's one now, tattering midair, and there again.
I'd dream entire episodes for her, I promise, whole glossy
sequences that unreel like film and last out small eternities.
But she wants only salt and birds with pretty names.

As for me, I'd run out of words surely as our late summer
thunderstorms gave over to unabated blasts of mistral.
My garden will dry, earth's surface cracked. Within days,
the topsoil grows parched as a desert floor.

But I read this as a signal to return with a handful
of barley seeds, back to those abandoned terraces,
following the line between the dead oak woods on one side,
orchards of almond, cherry, and apricot on the other.

I'll scatter barley seed and soon the early-autumn rains efface
each crusted-over rut, choke their small crevices running
fast with silt. Thin pennants of rose-gold spikes
will point to what's beneath.

What Late at Night He Wants from Eve

Inseparable—you know this—yet you drag me to the brink
of your mouth, the ripple that is your skin and the ripple
beneath your skin. I'll wait for you where the sigh
joins bone as in the old days inside the earth,

from there, follow the length of every newer world,
serve up that "us" you think so much of—mossy
and numb with want—so you can rest your knees
here in the seven downfalls of the infinite slope,

and so they hurt us less. You die with laughter and shake
with pleasure, in tremor. Offer the puffed friedcake, flour
with butter, with butter. You're teasing the peasant in me
who never forgets on waking to kiss your mouth, each breast,

each breast again, please oh truculent God, thus days
of this insist leading this poor man through the wilderness
with his useless eyes of the alien vigil, and you listen
while I hum my bubblings over, or wait still—

wait until there's almost nothing missing—
and my heart ignites with wanting and the grasses bend
and turn to gold, and time breaks free its mortal leash,
illusions singe my beard, and something bends my knee.

The Locust Eaters

Look! Zest of double helix, puff of genes.
Pureed pokeberry roots and flower of pimpernel
to boost the confidence—later, poultices of eyebright,
witch grass to stench the pride grown thick as adder's tongue.

And the monosyllables leaking from your lips? I sainted one tribe
to explain mistakes with facile grace. That ought to be enough.
Doe-eyed and vacant as morning fog, arms steel-studded, faces
blanched, ablaze, I set you out, and I loved most the new music
in your mouths—until you botched the names of things.

Languages lifted up like bobbers: Brahui, Teleg, Uzbek,
Lolo, Bata, Mono, Bug—Dravidian tongues, exotica in Malabo-Polynesian,
Tibetan grunts for cold—idioms globed as baubles.

Even the animals of dream turned away their heads.
But confound the plagues!
Whole meadows of flame leapt the summit of your little hill.
O bliss, the banner! The bugle! And one more for the Beagle!

I give it all to you—dogs, dolphins and gleaming brass, veers
of chasms & last, the trill of icicles against the winter stars.

Adam, Man of the World

Than this, there's but the unobstructed silence:
no announcements, too early, the conductor still slow over his coffee,
though already his fourth trip today—the river and back again—
wishing for a sail or oars, pours, ors, glancing twenty stories up

at a too high window, his face opening or closing, his mouth
opening and closing, and me, maybe I stopped wishing
the day I saw what lay outside the garden. How vast it was,
how small my painful shoes, how fast the apple lost its small appeal.

Oh, deserved. I'll take lunch today away from the office.
Noon recital in the atrium, let's say, a quartet for the unappointed.
Or still myself in the cool of the old synagogue, insists
nothing of its convictions. No music, no icons, no one.

We enter the tunnel: I know by the changed light.
This is a loaded moment, I say to this changeling soul.
Restive thing, there's the morning paper.
Mourning. Adorning. I must be reading it, though

if I read it again surely I'd remember nothing more than this:
everywhere they wish I'd done a better job.
Seems almost no doing of mine.
Nor the body, once mine, now station, coffee, train, street, shoe.

The apple, a bit shinier, just fits the briefcase.
Conductor says this time what he's wanted all his life to say.

Adam, Role Model

I tried it once. Tuxedo. Cummerbund. Black tie. I clean up well for a new man. I like to mingle, share a program, a concerto, glass of champagne at the interval. One, jade eyes, said she'd leave her husband if I took her to the parade in Nice, *La Bataille des Fleurs.*

Well, you know what that means. Flower tossing and families, soldiers, policemen, priests and punks—grubby youths—sneering and dirty. I set her up with Cain.

As the papers promised, mimosa had newly bloomed. Military bands with massed bugles marched, skinny fox-faced girls in pretty dresses flung petals and flowers torn from floats. Nasturtiums grew wherever there was space enough

and light, flowing like a bride's train toward the rocky beach where a group of elderly Italians lived on *grappa al mirtillo* and anise cookies in one of the gazebos. But the language proved insurmountable.

A sign on the beach warned of something—trawlers, strawberries, nudists—they couldn't tell.

In Corsica they washed and folded their few clothes, watched an Arab fill his writing pad from right to left with stems and curls while a young girl cut his silver hair and both drank thick coffee from cups with looped handles too small for the fingers of legends.

Night Bird Beneath Yellow Moon in Fog with Possibility

Adam grabs the fogged-in yellow moon, pockets it, large, some spruce,
larger, brushed blue with blue needles, short and blunt, he figures, why,
there's Goth enough here to last the night, but not

enough to make up what he's missing, nor to make the missing right, as
the night bird, hear her? figures what to eat, so there's an edge, which is nice.

The clock is blind, so that's nicer.

These are the years he makes up. At any moment he might cry out.
He has thought about it.

The red wine chills too fast under the yellow moon by the ocean in the fog.
There's that.

Look at his face, his hands, the lines in them. Tonight, more sky than usual
above the fog. Here, there is no light—none from the house,
none from the street, a long way through the reeds and cattails and on it,
no cars, and in them, no people—they are tending their own fires, or they sleep.

Only one stands so still you would not think him real.

God of Reprieve and Other Small Miracles

> *Let her finish her dance,*
> *Let her finish her dance.*
> *Ah dancer, ah, sweet dancer!*
> *—Yeats*

You can see her from the lake.
Maybe dawn in her sundress. Touch her.
You'll not want to be sorry for missing this.

Look. Smoke rises early from the huts
like the light backwash of comets, whitish, bluestained.
Say something to her. Say anything at all.

So, just whose still unravished bride is this?
I'm grinding rhino horn into my pocket for courage.
How it hurts, what morning wants, you think,
thinking it's the morning that wants anything at all.
Yet, were there hills, yea verily they'd skip like rams, no?

No? Don't argue. Maybe the dawn skips like rams,
maybe it is all yours, after all. All of it.
Be a little smug. What does it matter who knows?

Go on! It's me, begging myself.
It's me, hunting for the keys, uprooting the honey pot.
It's me, touched by the gold hand of having nothing gold.

It's me, hatched under the unborn wing of morning, son
of this orphan wing of night.
Here in our wilderness,
bathed here in our light and lake,
such sad monkeys.

The Fevered Chef Dreams in Menu

Seven days into my fast and already I'm dreaming in visions—
a pot of saxifrage honey, half empty on the table
two pages from Ecclesiastes push like early jonquils through the snow
a conference of third-tier regents goes informal at the Sheridan
and she at the bathroom mirror, braiding and unbraiding—

We'd made reservations for a battalion of sleepless—
a feast on board the signal ship to put the chef herself to ruin.
Those enchanted quail *en croute*, rich in their sauce.
Here, let me tell the others what happens when you see
as if from a distance yourself at the bathroom mirror,
braiding and unbraiding, braiding—

Or saved at that moment, you arrived in the city—
When I say you, this time I mean the one I can't help having
extraordinary thing, this business of can't help having,
as fêtes of Biblical proportion, as courses ecclesiastic,
as the holy smoke tears into the mutton, as the chef
at the bathroom mirror, braiding and unbraiding—

The chill mist collected on the camera lens, remember?
And the cold sea, the pale, icy cliffs where the world drew
inexplicably to dedication—is that true?
What do you think? When I say "you"
I mean of course, you, with me in this vision.

Moi, Easter Island

Those monoliths, austere-faced sentinels, giants broach the hills above the
tide line, give their backs to the Pacific. That's right, they face inland in their
petulance, mouths pursed, wanting not to know.

What nights through grim lips do they say to one another? These old Easter
Islanders with their Rongorongo script, the only written language in Oceania.

Here, for example, Figure 15, glyphs in triad from the "Santiago Staff,"
translated (more or less): "All the birds copulated with fish, there issued
forth the sun." It's night they must talk, and whatever it is they say, it lasts—
enough to think on for each of the daylight hours.

I'm fairly sure they say nothing to each other when the sky is blue and
cloudless, while the sun issues forth from land and fish.

Oddly, in Figure 17, a procreation item on the "Santiago Staff" repeats on
tablet, but lacks the phallic suffix on the X glyph.

Try, "Rongorongo." It's fun to say. I know how test pilots felt about the X glyph
—its absence—the need to have whatever's missing, to point the jet's nose
straight through the thinnest part of sky and leave the atmosphere behind,

escape velocity, the home orb glowing small beneath, the smaller ball
rounding until it is only another blue disk afloat in a field of black.

Wives and children growing smaller, continents hanging like pieces of cloth
on the line, shrinking until there's nothing left of the world but a weight in
center of gravity.

A child. A favorite chair. A plant you forgot to water.

Things fall back to earth at a predictable rate. Pilots know this, thirty two feet
per second squared. "Until maximum velocity is reached," is the stoic face
it wears in fat physics books I refuse to carry home.

So fast that the ocean's surface may as well be volcanic rock.
So fast, you might prefer to face the other way.

Puerto Ayora

We moved on the only inhabited port village in the Galápagos, found the Darwin Research Station where they keep the giant tortoises, including fabled "Lonesome George," who refuses from incompatible DNA or simple surliness to tango with any of the saturnine fillies flown in for his delight.

We bought the obligatory tee shirts ("I Love Boobies") and took pictures of exotic trees in exotic blossom. Then, in the fading darkness, boarded the small launches—*pangas*—at the quay.

I want to say masts were quickly stepped, sails unfurled in the placid of the coral lagoon, that wind-filled and ghost-white they rounded leeward, scattered in all directions across the fishing banks.

But we had only to yank the engine cord and motor back to our Yugoslav vessel of ancient vintage. The breeze and salt spray felt good on the sunburn, and I forgot, as I always did, to cover my camera lens, so the photos are dotted with droplets.

The ship had hired a port-side combo (bass, drums, guitars, flutes, and bells, percussion instruments made from formerly living things) for a soirée on the top deck, to watch the last of the sunset.

The Galápagos guides, comely Veronique and heartthrob Alejo, danced and sang native songs while the smallest musician chanted "fuck fucka fucka man" in percussive counterpoint.

Sunk into our lethargy, engines started up, water rushing past, though the ship stayed in place, or so it seemed. Here's what mattered—

those evening hours, unless you count mornings or the midday walks, or the late night wake-up with the late night hard-on, someone's voice in dream trailing "get de sail, man, quick," and that little engine of a voice drumming "fuck fucka fucka man."

Midnight, all manner of sea monster, the upper deck deserted and cool. Shark fins, dolphins, flightless cormorants fishing, manta rays leaping, twisting silver in the moonlight. And stars.

Oh stars, falling through their frigid fire to the deserted rail.

Palo Santo Tree, Galápagos

Two denuded trees call to the same mockingbird—the tree on the right spreading its arms in welcome, the left one trying to lay its head on your breast—and we want to be born.

Three rays leap clear of the Pacific, twisting and spinning so to teach Balanchine a thing or two about arabesques: their black backs glittering triangles and salmon bellies shining silver, they smack the water hard, as one, and float down and down with their prize of captured sun.

Do they, too, want to be weightless, as my little boy who masters the shallows with mask and snorkel, hunting the blue-eyed damsel fish or Moorish idol? I think not.

I think the rays are appeasable, satisfied with their blazing wings, their zone of grace. Neither devil nor any god ever felt so little hurt.

I could say that a column of fire illumines Christmas Eve in the islands, voiceless, all wind and spent heat, no form, no face, but for a starry finger pointed at the small space between two small trees—palo santo—night stick—of the family, frankincense and myrrh.

I could say the palo santo tree leafs on Christmas day, and I would be right, but who would believe me, even if a fresh wound falls each night from each palo santo, like an autumn leaf. Look, says the birder beside me—out there past the pelican—a wandering tattler, just the back of his head, all black, see him?

Very rare.

Iguassu

Track one, the intertidal zone, bright sun—
someone's legs over legs, mouth to shoulder blade,
ionized trace of aurora borealis a half-breath away wisps
static rustle across a single speaker
and a soprano sax lingers on a rim of cloud.

Bright pinging and corrugated shuffle
from the kitchen door, slow urge—
Tenochtitlan mounded at the epicenter.

There goes the modern exorcist
with his bells and cloak. Tattered cloak.

Everything burned, his earthly wares bequeathed
to a skiff and sunk to the river bottom
to consort with mollusks.

What's left?

What's left, says the guide, can be found
at the westward terminal,
Ciudad del Espirito Santo,

a small stained aperture of syllables
forming perfect homes, cathedrals, hotels with frescoes,
courtyards, everything. Even busses to the waterfall.

The sharp sun, out of breath, slips
to its knees on the cinder track—

stark astral for the ladder and short stretch.
All mouth and shoulder blades.
Near waterfall drumming.

Iguassu, seen already in the travelogues.
I know that sound, borealis, washing out
the eaves and flues. No sleep, no first ring
of purgatory. No rings at all.

I know the night heals.
I know where there are chords
like southern jungles filled with hissing octaves,
faint harmonics, languid stones.

Thé Dansant

See her down there? Our planet as a child—
red, eruptive, difficult, Jurassic, lost.
At Olduvai Gorge, a flat-headed chunk of skull gathers
in the fetid air, one millennium into another.

Near Lake Turkana, the twelve-year-old who went for water
two million years ago—whose narrow brow still lards the plain.
Jaw fragments, leg and hand bones. A scattering
of hackberry seeds. Teeth. Those, too.
It got cold, then colder. You see?

One night the moon diminished, next the sun.
Still, we forgive the lightning, promise children light follows night.
What do we know? It pleases us to think it might.
Let it be so, as it pleased the kids to dream *thele,*
dream *thelyblast,* dream the lee wash of night itself.

Only an epoch pause, each of us
a furrowed, hair-matted thing,
staring at the ice-borne rim just long enough
to scatter seeds across the melt.

IV

♓

Orpheus Ascending

I. Orpheus and Eurydice Take Italian Lessons

Orpheus is doing his own thinking now.

Quella ragazza è molto bella!
That girl is very beautiful.

Eurydice has feelings, too.
"Maurizio is from Verona."
"We are Italians."
"The banana is yellow."

Partiamo stasera.
Let's leave this evening.
This is Eurydice's thought. Pop six discs
in the cd player. Power of suggestion.

Pack, notify the credit card companies,
take the dog to the pound, check the expiration date
on the passport, your roots are showing.

⤙

In Venice, there's a mud bath, a good shoemaker,
a respectable hairdresser (*un buon parrucchiere*).

The word for grapes, *uva*, is always singular, never plural.
Orpheus and Eurydice agree that this is, somehow, deep.

Italian has a tense for the past, and another for
the long past, *Il Passato Remoto*, the "Past Absolute."
This, too, seems to them significant.

Three months of intense study, now Orpheus
can order his favorite dish at La Strega,
watch Fellini films without glancing at the subtitles,
understand what his future in-laws are saying about him
while they smile and wipe the tomato sauce from their lips.

Both understand the idea behind Mimi's tortured heart in *La Bohème*.
They sound sexy, sound pretty smart.

Enthralled by ancient burial rites,
Eurydice must visit the catacombs.
Not afraid of dark, moldy tunnels, she loves the sound
of bats, has always been intrigued by bones, skulls,
preserved body parts.

Assured, she won't lose herself in the labyrinth
of passages and chambers that once held the remains
of early Christian martyrs. It's another hot day.
Catacombs—great way to cool off.

↳

Orpheus loves driving.
There's only one car named Ferrari and he knows
there's nothing practical about driving a car made for speed,
but wants leather gloves that stretch tight over the knuckles,
sunglasses like goggles, a supermodel in the passenger seat.
Or Eurydice. Okay, Eurydice, but the sexy one
from *Black Orpheus*, with Jobim's bossa novas
and ah, that Marpessa Dawn.

Eurydice prefers to walk.
She'll buy something comfortable in Florence.
She wants to stroll past the limpid waters
of Venice's canals, hike the Appian Way, check out
the ruins of Pompeii, where in 79 A.D., Vesuvius buried
2000 people under a layer of dust, lava, and stone.

Orpheus considers photojournalism. More than anything
he wants to wear khaki and carry several cameras around his neck
as he searches for Eurydice, waits for that candid shot,
Eurydice emerging from dim light, say, or climbing
a steep flight of steps in a flowing gown, gauzy, pellucid.

He wants to fill a book with images of old women
hanging the laundry, or their husbands sitting on cane chairs
at the local bar, playing chess. He imagines stray tomcats,
a clowder, eating leftover spaghetti from a piece of newspaper
or young couples embracing along the Ponte Vecchio
for the first time, or the last.

They buy flash cards. They tune in Italian TV
at night, radio stations at the office, buy Italian products:
espresso machines, hair driers, rice and fruits.

Together, they read the fine print
in the owners' manuals to learn technical terms,
they read Verdi libretti, practice saying, "La Scala"
until they say it like natives. Like Milanese.

Practical people, they set realistic goals,
learn grammar, practice rolling their *r*'s in the shower.
They learn to their great delight
that Dante and Boccaccio both wrote in Italian.

ﮋ

A man comes to the door, tells Eurydice he's left
a *dizionario Italiano* in the subbasement
near the coal furnace, many flights down.
She can fetch it.

He wears a black coat, maybe a red lining, speaks
so very slowly she can make out every word, every wound.

Orpheus says he'll follow in a bit, bring his camera, a new Minolta
with telephoto lens and strobe light. He's delighted with the specs:

> *Camera type: 35mm SLR*
> *Viewfinder: SAR roof mirror*
> *Shutter type: Electronically controlled*
> *Focus type: Phase-detection system; multi metering with cross-hair type*
> *Rewind: Auto rewind (countdown display)*
> *Exposure modes: Portrait, landscape, close up, sports, night portrait,*
> *automatic, manual*

He's got plenty of film.

Peccato, peccato.

II. Orpheus Has Singing Lessons, Eurydice Assays Caving

Orpheus loves life, adores a song, worships a lyre.

Sure, Botticelli, Rafael, Caravaggio, Pisano,
Masaccio, Ghirlandaio, Sofia Loren, *bravo*,
they're great, so is Florence. Giotto,
vineyards, olive trees, *bravissimo*.
But hasn't Italy always been a song?

Orpheus runs his scales, arpeggios,
supports his voice from the diaphragm,
does his breathing exercises
lying down, a heavy book on his belly.

Sing *luna*, sing *una*, sing *cubo, lupo, tuo*.
Sing *serpente*, thou snake. Sing *serpente pazzo*. Thou crazy snake!
Damn your green poisons.
Clearly, the situation is serious.

Orpheus summons forth a chorus of shepherds and nymphs
outside the entrance to the catacombs
with a list of Neopolitan songs for his beloved.

Ecco! Beloved! Name your song! Name your country!
Cinese, inglese, francese,
tedesco, greco, indiano,
irlandese, giapponese, coreano,
messicano, polacco, russo,
spagnolo, svizzero—

Eurydice can't get enough of caverns, grottoes.

His voice is a golden hand,
a charm wound around my breasts,
his throat is a pure summer of eggplant.
Eurydice would think this, if only she heard his song.

She can't. In the caverns, her heart tolls softly.
She remembers breaking the legs
of her black horse in the woods at night,
as delirium welled from his livid eyes.

There, doesn't get much more *de profundis* than this,
sing the shepherds and the nymphs.

When they get the idea, and they'll get it soon,
Orpheus can sing: oh angel, oh empyrean.
Gotta song, gotta voice, got *cuore*.
Got Isidore Ducasse, Comte de Lautréamont
for bedtime reading.

Gotta look back, O, those barbarians,
gotta look back, O, these brown arms
your whole horizon.
Orpheus unslings the Minolta.
Load, flip to automatic.
Exposure modes: portrait, landscape, close up.
Night portrait, *ecco la!*, that's the one,
rolled *r*'s, flash.

Countdown display, pellucid.

Peccato, peccato.

III. Kill Me a Red-Hipped Humblebee Atop a Thistle

Very near, but unembraced, your almost human face.
"Coward, why com'st thou not?"
If you loved me. You would.

What was it Mrs. Franklin said to Ben?
He kissed her, sailed to France with his
Philadelphia Poor Richard's French,
fingers tingling from the lightning bolt?

If you loved me more?

There's the Fatenbenefratelli,
a hospital founded by the monks in 1548
on Isola Tiberina, that pretty
ship-shaped island in the Tiber
where they nursed the wounded and the dying
during the siege of Rome.

God, if you loved me more.

No, one cannot always remember exactly why
one has been happy, but as Auden said,
there's no forgetting that one was.

First thing to know, Eurydice, she says,
"Italian Cooking" doesn't exist.
It's all regional: Venice, Naples, Sicily.
Mid-central New Jersey, olive-less.
Gothic New England, God,
if only you loved me more.
No, put away the Italian dictionary.
Stash the Arabic for Beginners.

Ni'ma—blessing, gift.
Qishr—peal, crust.
Lubab—marrow, best part.
Forget them.

Be kind toward the wayfarer. Model sentences.
Lesson Seventeen.
You'd put it away if you loved me.

Confession: I cannot bear to part with the wildflowers
I pressed for you, that have grown faces and fingers,
that have become you.

The houses we return to in dream do not permit description.
The frothing of the hedges I keep deep inside me.
Thoreau engraved the fields in his soul.
Mapped them there.

But tell me about the rooms.
Was the garret cluttered, the nook warm?
How was it lighted? The kitchen, was it filled
with intoxicants—spices, cakes?

And where was silence found?
The marrow, the wayfarer, the best part.
If you loved, oh God, me, you'd stay.

IV. Old Terminal, Rome

Eurydice and Orpheus have their first-class tickets
from Roma to Turin, have their small Chiantis
at the station bar, their smokes, Italian TV on mute,
by coincidence *Orfeo, Il Giorno Prima,* a short,
and Venditti on the loud speakers,
they make out the word *città,* loud,
sounds like he's been doing sambuca shots
with a little grappa for texture.

And it's Caruso right there on the stool.
Gotta be him! The hair. The profile.
The black coat. Hat.
Orpheus wants a few pointers on breath control.
We just missed, says Eurydice.

But Orpheus doesn't buy it.
Everybody's a prophet, a world-full
of wannabe seers.

No, Baby, no. Here we are. A fast *pendolino*
leaves at noon—*mezzogiorno*—dining
car smack in the middle, checked tablecloths,
white china with cerulean rims,
il scontrino, the luggage tag, in his fist.

We almost didn't, but we missed.
Just.

Might as well imagine we're in Schenectady
as Rome, the three of us, you, me—
Enrico here—gotta be Caruso, sitting between us.

Caruso rolls himself a smoke just like
Marcello Mastroianni in 1961 as Nello Poletti
in *Ladykiller of Rome*,
then lip synchs some "O Sole Mio,"
"Ritorna a Sorrento"—one of those Neopolitan songs.

Now he thinks we're his love birds,
he smooths our breast feathers through the cage
with his yellowed fingers.

Eurydice tells Orpheus the truth.
This quintessence of dramatic tenors,
this amalgam of Italian *amore*
imagines we're content to wait
while we imagine how our love imagines us
and Rome steams in and out in black and white,
like so many pigeons in the Piazza di Spagna.

Hey, the Italian lessons are paying dividends already.
There's time, an hour, maybe more.
Someone's peppering the station with announcements—

departures, arrivals, cities named for all the elements
of the periodic table, even the unstable ones,
spices too, and a litany of middling saints.

Still, the words tumble out of their corner boxes,
all the syllables in a string, shank-hafted
and crackling like crows,
something about looking back
or not looking back, hard to say,

sounds like an oracle, sounds like a libretto,
sounds gnostic, sounds like a warning,
sounds like chant, serious chant—
sounds like city after city swallowed whole.

Eurydice fixes his tie, so what, Roman silk,
soft, striped, understated.

They insist on taunting us this way, promises,
marshy, wet, permeable, how does that movie go?
Swept away . . . by an unusual destiny in the blue sea of August—

Gennarino . . .

Orpheus orders a plate of olives,
some Tuscan bread, extra virgin oil from Modena,
light as the wings of Sicilian saints in summer,
in his pocket the faith healer's business card.

He wipes clean the camera lens, takes a reading.
Plenty of light.
Winds through the f-stops like a Ferrari
dreaming in hairpin, going on feel.
Winds though them again.

He wants to know if it's true.
Eurydice knows the odds.

Gauze. Pellucid.

Gone.

Slow film.

Peccati. Peccati.

V

♓

The Herbalist

Next life, I'll devote to the earnest pursuit of languor.
A dubious sort, I'll live like a Buddha, impervious, fat.
What a relief to flout unknowable accounts—
let the earth offer up its sober charities if it wants.
Moses strikes the rock and brings forth the bubbling stream.
We get to swim in it, lie down in it, do what we want.
Want. The thing unfurls like tight-packed knots
of fiddlehead fern, mandrakes, gentian, garden spurge,
opening large upon themselves, stopless, filling the sky.
Let whatever we find turn to seeds, jackbeans, stalks
uplifted, rattle like brittlebush in a dry wind while years lock
into years, and contentment fills the mouth.

Drought &

a pair of ginko trees wither on the dry creek's banks,
below, bare rocks expose themselves in the fissured bed,

an embarrassment of private parts, where an old man
with a fringe of hair, rod and reel, pants rolled—

not bothering to cast—only stands as his wife waits,
her face the knotted grace of driftwood, & above

on a leafless willow branch, a crow, its wings flecked
with purple constellations, like iridescent bruises, spindles

from one claw to the other as if to say how dull we are
with drought, how the dead & living blur & the walls cover

themselves with calligraphy & rooms, relics, friezes, music,
whole nights of mystic chords ring through the loft

where a dancer works combinations—wet slap of bare feet
against bare floor, *jetés, glissades, arabesques* & odd

off-center *pliés,* arms stretched out into the mirrored wall,
body arched against the heat, she strains an hour, two, then

a grapefruit, her rib cage glazed with sweat and salt, hip, thigh,
usurping idly—who will say how long

she has nor any of us, not a single clue out
where the slow static of power lines, brittle, metallic,

mingle with the crow's defiant cries, sleepless too,
this bird—eyes lidless, moon-dry, white.

Entering this room,

you can't help thinking, I am a set of orchid vases, or the orchids
themselves, clustered and supplicating.

I am, you think, one-quarter handblown glass—enough to set for six
guests or ten. Surely this part of me was fired in the Philippines then
cooled in the rain by women who despite their age were not unused to dance.

I am velum, I think, for dreaming, I am rice pearls strung and clasped with a
silver heart in place of the old one, worn, grown tired and better off this way.

I woe-is-me before the you must leave the room, now thought, you think,
leave it now—too dangerous, you think, it is too,

you think, much of you.

Plus Pijouns

Creation by committee. Inevitable meetings with desultory angels,
long hours, stale coffee. This one had a unique vision of the watery world:
mollusks, coral, half-plant, half-animal anemones.

Adrift. Moving from one spongy form to another.
Endless sequence of identical reflections.
As with lovers, moving from one apartment to the next,
one lover to another. No, more than drifted.

A break for errands. Retracing steps to that errant catalogue
of cloud formations. That distinct autonomy of theirs.
Trip to the promontory to glean stray bits of falling light,
like the last ripened fruits.

And pigeons. *Pijouns.*

In history to come, some interview peasants, blacksmiths, country priests.
The local pronunciation of a particular phoneme or slight syntactic
variation.

Timeworn, wind-worn dictum. *Plus pijouns.*

In that last hour, a billion vacant bedrooms, swept clean,
shutters opened, shelves emptied.
Vases for all the flowers to come.

December, no flowers yet. And no small drop of spirits.

There are days even the first Man wants no more than to
milk goat cheese at those churning wheels
in a farmhouse with a single corkscrew of blue smoke rising
from a chimney pot. No history.

Here's where you might want to incarnate Eve.
Walk with her beside the scythes, sickles, plowshares.
Let her, for example, exult in a sylvan scent.

Morning, hear her bathing. Facial cream over that tall, mineral
forehead of hers. The granular brown of her repeated,
self-searching glances.

A nearly hallucinatory presence filling the radiant oval.

Let's suppose a language. Gallo-Romanic breath relics.
Words circulate like precious currency, evanescent gold.

Char. An entire lexicon devoted to nothing but grain.
More char. Promise me out loud, she demands, this Eve.
Your mind on the moon, you sign anything she gives you.

Snowdust. Woodsmoke. Like you.
With Magdalene's hand you measure altitude.
Bless you, she says, over and over again.

Meaning nothing spiritual.
Meaning the harm is washed away.

Notes to Orpheus Ascending

Black Orpheus, *Orfeu Negro* (1959), in Portuguese, directed by Marcel Camus, a retelling of the Orpheus and Eurydice myth, set during Carneval in Rio de Janiero. Marpessa Dawn played Eurydice to Breno Mello's Orfeo. The soundtrack by Antonio Carlos Jobim introduced bossa nova to the rest of the world. Spectacular cinematography by Jean Bourgoin.

Peccato means sin or shame.

Cuore means heart.

Isidore Ducasse (1846-1870), pen name Comte de Lautréamont, poet, novelist and short story writer, is noted most for *Chants de Maldorer* and *The Second Book of Decadence*.

Luchino Visconti (1906-1976), Italian director of *The Innocent, Death in Venice, The Stranger, The Leopard*, and *Rocco and His Brothers*.

Antonin Artaud (1896-1948), French theorist, philosopher, playwright and madman. In response to an article on Van Gogh, Artaud wrote, "No one has ever written, painted, sculpted, modeled, built or invented except literally to get out of hell."

Christoph Willibald Gluck (1714-1787), born in Erasbach, settled in Vienna in 1752 as Kapellmeister of the Prince of Saxe-Hildburghausen's orchestra. In 1762, composed the opera *Orfeo ed Euridice*, the first of his so-called "reform operas."

Karl Ditters von Dittersdorf (1739-1799), Austrian composer and close friend of Mozart. Particularly affecting is his Requiem in C Minor.

Marguerite Yourcenar (1903-1987), French novelist, essayist, and short story writer, gained international fame with her historical novels in which she drew psychologically penetrating portraits of figures from the distant past. Among her best known works are *Memoirs of Hadrian*, *Coup de Grâce*, and *Oriental Tales*. Yourcenar, who settled in the U.S. at the outbreak of World War II and taught at Sarah Lawrence College in New York, became the first woman to be elected to the Académie Française.

Humblebee is a bumblebee. The section title is taken from Shakespeare, *A Midsummer Night's Dream*, Act IV, Scene I. Bottom:

> *Mounsieur Cobweb, good mounsieur, get you your*
> *weapons in your hand, and kill me a red-hipped*
> *humble-bee on the top of a thistle; and, good*
> *mounsieur, bring me the honey-bag.*

Fatenbenefratelli means, literally, the do-good brothers.

Orfeo, Il Giorno Primo is a 1995 Italian short film directed by Giovanni Minerba.

A *pendolino* is a very fast Eurostar train.

Città means, of course, city.